STAR BIOGRAPHIES

DWAYNE JOHNSON

Fly!
An Imprint of Abdo Zoom
abdobooks.com

KENNY ABDO

abdobooks.com

Published by Abdo Zoom, a division of ABDO, P.O. Box 398166, Minneapolis, Minnesota 55439. Copyright © 2019 by Abdo Consulting Group, Inc. International copyrights reserved in all countries. No part of this book may be reproduced in any form without written permission from the publisher. Fly!™ is a trademark and logo of Abdo Zoom.

Printed in the United States of America, North Mankato, Minnesota.
092018
012019

 THIS BOOK CONTAINS RECYCLED MATERIALS

Photo Credits: Alamy, AllWrestlingSuperstars.com, Getty Images, Icon Sportswire, newscom, Shutterstock, ©John Barrett/photolink/mediapunch/Shutterstock p12 ©Kristina Bumphrey/Shutterstock p20
Production Contributors: Kenny Abdo, Jennie Forsberg, Grace Hansen
Design Contributors: Dorothy Toth, Neil Klinepier

Library of Congress Control Number: 2018946309

Publisher's Cataloging-in-Publication Data

Names: Abdo, Kenny, author.
Title: Dwayne Johnson / by Kenny Abdo.
Description: Minneapolis, Minnesota : Abdo Zoom, 2019 | Series: Star biographies | Includes online resources and index.
Identifiers: ISBN 9781532125447 (lib. bdg.) | ISBN 9781641856898 (pbk) | ISBN 9781532126468 (ebook) | ISBN 9781532126970 (Read-to-me ebook)
Subjects: LCSH: Johnson, Dwayne, 1972- --Juvenile literature. | Actors--United States--Biography--Juvenile literature. | Wrestlers--Biography--Juvenile literature. | Motion picture actors and actresses--Biography--Juvenile literature.
Classification: DDC 791.43028092 [B]--dc23

TABLE OF CONTENTS

DWAYNE JOHNSON

Ruling the wrestling ring and the **silver screen**, Dwayne Johnson has fought his way to becoming one of Hollywood's most popular stars.

Johnson's climb to fame began with "The Rock," a popular wrestling character. Then he took Hollywood by storm starring in today's biggest movies.

EARLY YEARS

Dwayne Douglas Johnson was born in Hayward, California, in 1972.

Oregon

Idaho

Nevada

Utah

HAYWARD

CALIFORNIA

Arizona

His father, Rocky Johnson, and grandfather, "High Chief" Peter Maivia, were both professional wrestlers.

Johnson lived in New Zealand and Hawaii while growing up. At 18, he was offered a **scholarship** to play defensive tackle at the University of Miami.

THE BIG TIME

After college, Johnson joined the Canadian Football team, the Calgary Stampeders. He was cut two months into the season. He only had seven dollars in his bank account.

Johnson **trained** with his father to become a professional wrestler. He fought in a few **matches** under the name Flex Kavana. Johnson made his World Wrestling Entertainment (WWE) debut as Rocky Maivia in 1996.

In 1997, he joined the Nation of Domination as The Rock. With way more **victories** than losses, he quickly became a wrestling favorite.

Johnson started getting movie offers in 2000. He starred in *The Scorpion King* in 2002. Johnson made the *Guinness Book of World Records* as the highest paid first-time leading actor.

Johnson has starred in many **blockbusters** since. Movies like *Moana, Central Intelligence,* and *Jumanji: Welcome to the Jungle* have earned him major success.

LEGACY

Johnson founded the Dwayne Johnson Rock Foundation in 2006. It is a charity that works with children who are terminally ill.

FOUNDATION

Pay to the Order of: **The**

Two thousand

Palm

Las

www

Date: **June 15, 2008**

no Resort

NV

entheatres.com

k Foundation $ **2,500**

e hundred ⁰⁰/₁₀₀   Dollars

SKYSCR
PREMI

He became *Forbes Magazine's* highest paid actor in 2018. Johnson earned $124 million that year. A big leap from the seven dollars he started with.

GLOSSARY

blockbuster – a movie that is a big commercial success.

match – a competition in which wrestlers fight against each other.

scholarship – money or aid given to help a student continue their studies.

silver screen – another name for the movies.

terminally ill – being incurably sick.

train – learning a skill by a teacher or coach.

victory – defeating an opponent during a match.

ONLINE RESOURCES

Booklinks
NONFICTION NETWORK
FREE! ONLINE NONFICTION RESOURCES

To learn more about Dwayne Johnson, please visit abdobooklinks.com. These links are routinely monitored and updated to provide the most current information available.

INDEX